A New Duck

My First Look At
The Life Cycle of a Bird

Written by Pamela Hickman
Illustrated by Heather Collins

Kids Can Press

This is the park

where Paul plays.

Many wild birds live in parks.

Can you find these birds in the picture?

sparrow

Mallard

crow

woodpecker

swallow

starling

nuthatch

These are the ducks
that swim in the park
where Paul plays.

In early spring, Mallards choose
their mates and fly to their
nesting grounds.

Together, they look for a well-
hidden place to build a nest,
usually near water.

A male Mallard is called a drake.
His bright colors help him
attract a mate.

A female Mallard is called a hen.

This is the nest
that was built by the ducks,
that swim in the park
where Paul plays.

Male and female Mallards cooperate at nest-building time. While the drake watches for enemies, the hen builds the nest with grass and reeds. She lines it with down feathers that she plucks from her breast.

Barn Swallow

Other birds build different kinds of nests.

Baltimore Oriole

Hairy Woodpecker

Marsh Wren

These are the eggs
that were laid in the nest,
that was built by the ducks,
that swim in the park
where Paul plays.

The Mallard hen lays one egg a day until she has a clutch of 8 to 12 eggs. Then she sits on them to keep them warm until they hatch. This is called incubation.

28 days

The drake flies to a larger lake or marsh, where he spends the summer with other male ducks.

These are the ducklings
that hatched from the eggs,
that were laid in the nest,
that was built by the ducks,
that swim in the park
where Paul plays.

Newly hatched ducklings are covered with down feathers that help keep them warm.

A few hours after the ducklings have hatched, the mother leads them to water and shows them what plants and insects to eat.

These are the fledglings
that grew from the ducklings,
that hatched from the eggs,
that were laid in the nest,
that was built by the ducks,
that swim in the park
where Paul plays.

Month-old ducklings lose their down and grow new feathers. This is called molting.

At two months, the young ducks are called fledglings. Their strong flight feathers have grown in, their wings have developed, and they are learning to fly.

These are the new ducks
that grew from the fledglings,
that grew from the ducklings,
that hatched from the eggs,
that were laid in the nest,
that was built by the ducks,
that swim in the park
where Paul plays.

As summer ends, new Mallards join other ducks on large lakes and marshes.

They spend their days fattening up on plants and insects, storing energy for the long flight ahead.

See you in the spring!

In fall, most Mallard ducks fly, or migrate, in flocks to a warmer place to spend the winter.

Some Mallards may stay around all year where there is food and open water.

Note to Parents

The life cycle of a Mallard duck is an example of how one kind of bird grows from egg to adult. Ducks, geese and pheasants are precocial birds, which means that their newly hatched babies are covered with feathers and can walk and feed themselves within a few hours. Most common garden birds, such as starlings and jays, are altricial birds. When altricial birds hatch, they have no feathers. Their parents feed them and keep them warm in the nest for several weeks.

Children are delighted when they see baby birds, whether it's ducklings in the park or robins in the backyard. Your family can attract birds to your home by setting out a birdbath or birdfeeder. You can also make a simple birdhouse for sparrows, wrens or swallows using a large empty milk carton. For the entrance, cut a hole one inch (2.5 cm) in diameter just below the bend on one side of the rinsed-out carton. You'll need two small holes on the other side with a wire threaded through for attaching the birdhouse to a pole or tree. Use waterproof tape to keep the top of the carton tightly closed. To help attract nesting birds, line the bottom of the carton with grass, dry leaves or bits of yarn or string. If a pair of birds moves into the birdhouse, your family can watch them raise their young. Enjoy the birds without disturbing them, and they may return to your garden year after year to raise new families.

Text copyright © 1999 by Pamela Hickman
Illustrations copyright © 1999 by Heather Collins/Glyphics

We acknowledge the support of the Canada Council for the Arts and the
Ontario Arts Council for our publishing program.

Published in Canada by
Kids Can Press Ltd.
29 Birch Avenue
Toronto, ON M4V 1E2

Published in the U.S. by
Kids Can Press Ltd.
85 River Rock Drive, Suite 202
Buffalo, NY 14207

The artwork in this book was rendered in watercolor and gouache.

Edited by Linda Biesenthal
Designed by Blair Kerrigan/Glyphics
Printed in Hong Kong by Wing King Tong Co. Ltd.

CM 99 0 9 8 7 6 5 4 3 2 1

Canadian Cataloguing in Publication Data

Hickman, Pamela

A new duck : my first look at the life cycle of a bird

ISBN 1-55074-613-8

1. Birds — Life cycles — Juvenile literature. I. Collins, Heather. II. Title

QL676.2.H535 1999   j571.8'18   C98-932225-4